RUUP4IT?

ltle bk

of

d8s

WAN2HELP?

We are constantly updating our files of text messages and emoticons for the next edition of this and our other text message books. If you would like to add variations of your own please e-mail us at

jokes@michaelomarabooks.com

We will let you know if your additions are going to be included. Thank you

RUUP4IT?

ltle bk

of txt

d8s

First published in Great Britain in 2001 by
Michael O'Mara Books Limited
9 Lion Yard
Tremadoc Road
London SW4 7NQ

A CIP catalogue record for this book is available from the British Library

ISBN 1-85479-892-8

5 7 9 10 8 6 4

Devised and compiled by Gabrielle Mander

Cover Design: Design 23
Telephone supplied and used by kind permission of Motorola

Designed and typeset by Design 23

www.mombooks.com

Made and printed in Great Britain by William Clowes, Beccles, Suffolk

CONTENTS

RUUP4IT?
Making friends on the move

Picture this: you've fancied him or her for ages but you don't want to walk up and say 'Here I am, the girl (or guy) of your dreams.' Flirting on the move can be fun, and now there is faster, easier, smarter way to do it with *RUUP4IT?*

All you need is access to a mobile phone or email, and his or her mobile number. This little book has over a thousand of the best attention-grabbing lines ever; some in-your-face and some so subtle that you can test his or her intelligence at the same time. Emoticons can spice up the conversation too, using punctuation marks and symbols to tell others what you think of them at a stroke.

All mobile phones vary, but access to the messaging service is usually simple. Go to **'Menu'** and scroll to **'Messages'** then to **'Message Editor'**. Compose your message by using the letter and number keys on your phone. Each key represents more than one letter and symbol in both upper and lower case so you need to press repeatedly until the letter you want appears. Press the # key to stop the letter flashing. When your message is complete press **'ok'** and your message will be sent.

A few hints might be useful. The fewer characters that you use without spaces between words, the speedier and less expensive your message will be both to send and receive. Start each new word with a capital letter. A capital can mean a long sound.

A capital in the middle of a word can also mean a double letter: so **BAB = Baby** and **BuBle = Bubble**. A **$** sign means double **S** thus **SC$ = Success**. A full list of the basic shortcuts and abbreviations is given in **Bak2YaROts.**

Chatting up by phone is just for fun. Be safe, if you do want to take things further, don't go home alone with a stranger. Make a date to meet with friends in a club or pub, <u>**not**</u> your home. Trust your instincts and don't meet again if you have any doubts. Don't send obscene messages, and show your new friend respect. Be yourself, be creative, have fun with *RUUP4IT?* Well **RU?**

GeTYaC0t...
Get your coat, you've pulled – acronyms and abbreviations

AML	all my love
ATT	about time too
BBS	be back soon
BEG	big evil grin
CSG	chuckle, snicker, grin

CSThnknAU	can't stop thinking about you
CUIMD	see you in my dreams
CUL8R	see you later
CU2NITE@8@YaPlAc?	see you tonight at 8 at your place?
DYCHO	do you come here often?
FAS?	fancy a snog?
FEITNEdIM	feel the need in me
FMDIDGAD	frankly my dear, I don't give a damn

FYEO	for your eyes only
GetYaCOtUvPLd	get your coat, you've pulled
GMD?	get my drift?
GSOH	good salary, own home
GSOH	good sense of humour
Hot4U	hot for you
ILuvU	I love you

ImWUHBW4	I'm what you've been waiting for
INEdU2NITE	I need you tonight
INOUWanMe	I know you want me
ISU	it's so unfair
IWANU	I want you
KOTC	kiss on the cheek
KOTL	kiss on the lips

L8R later

LolLuvUWntUTLMeYaNAm?
hello, I love you won't you
tell me your name?

LolsItMeURLOkin4?
hello, is it me you're
looking for?

LtsMAKThsANite2Rmba
let's make this a night
to remember

MAkMyDASA+!
make my day, say yes

MTM/WOYD	meet the man of/woman of your dreams
NETMA	nobody ever tells me anything
NNWWSNM	nudge, nudge, wink, wink, say no more
OIC	oh I see
OWntUStAJst ALTleBitLnga?	oh won't you stay just a little bit longer?
PM	private message

QSLP	reply please
QSO	conversation
RMB	ring my bell
RSN	really soon now
SOHF	sense of humour failure
SYS	see you soon
TTFN	ta ta for now
TOY	thinking of you
TX	thanks

T2UL8r	talk to you later
U&MeL8r?LivTDrm	you and me later? Live the dream
UTlkin2Me?	you talking to me?
VVCAMCS?	voulez-vous couchez avec moi ce soir?
WICIWIW	what I see is what I want
WUSIWUG	what you see is what you get
YYSSW	yeah, yeah, sure, sure whatever

+! +! +!	YES! YES! YES!
-! -! -!	NO! NO! NO!
X	kiss
XMeQk	kiss me quick
Xoxoxoxo	hugs and kisses
YG	young gentleman
YL	young lady
* H *	hug
* WX *	wink
* X *	kiss

LoIsItMeURLOkin4?
Hello is it me you're looking for?

(-E:	I am the one in the corner wearing wearing bifocals
:-)8	I am the well-dressed girl by the bar
:-)-8	yes, I am a big girl
B*)	sure, the moustache and designer sunglasses are a retro statement!

=:-)	I am an older man/woman
:-)}	I think the goatee works
,.'v	I have short hair (profile)
,o'v	I have short hair (profile)
~o'v	I have a long fringe (profile)
?:-)	I have wavy hair, parted on the right
r:-)	I have a ponytail
@:-)	I have wavy hair

#:-)	I have tangled hair
&:-)	I have curly hair
@.'v	I have curly hair (profile)
?:)	I have a single curl of hair
5:-)	Elvis dead?
&:-]	I am very handsome with a square jaw
:-))	I have a double chin
:-#	I wear braces
:-{#}	I am wearing braces too

}:^#)	I have a pointy nose
*<8-)X	I am a party animal
(:-)	I am bald but sexy
:-{}	I am wearing lipstick
:-+	I may be wearing too much lipstick
:-) ,	I have an outie belly button
:-) .	I have an innie belly button
:-)^<	I am a big boy

:-)8<	I am a big girl
((Y))	I am a really big girl
:%)	I am an accountant
:?)	I am a philosopher
§;^()	I am a lawyer
&;-P	I am a suave guy on the make
{{-}}}	I'm a refugee from the '60s
:-)K-	I am wearing a shirt and tie

;-)}</////>	you could say I'm a corporate-type guy
l-(	I have lost my contact lenses. Do you want to help me look for them?
l:-)	just because I have a monobrow it doesn't mean I'm bad-tempered
O :-) @ <3	I am an angel (at heart, at least)
*<o'v	yeah, the hat is a fashion statement

:^)	I may not be good-looking but I have personality
:-Q ?	do you smoke?
:-Q	I smoke
:/i	no smokers need apply
:-) ... :-(... :-) ... :-(...	I do have these mood swings

IsThtAGnInYaPo KtOrRUJst Plezd2CMe?

21st Century chat-up lines

ALThosCrvs&MeWivNoBrks

      all those curves and me
      with no brakes

CnIBrw10p2CLYaMa2ThnkHr?

      can I borrow 10p to call
      your mother to thank
      her?

CnlChkYaShrtLbl2ClfURTRiteSlz?

        can I check your shirt
        label to see if you are
        the right size?

CnlChkYaShrtLbl2ClfUWerMdeInHvn?

        can I check your shirt
        label to see if you were
        made in heaven?

CnlFlrtWivU?   can I flirt with you?

CnlHavDrctns2Ya<3?

        can I have directions to
        your heart?

DdntICUOnTVLstNite?

didn't I see you on TV
last night?

DdntWeGo2DFrtSchls?

didn't we go to different
schools?

DdUHrtYasIfWenUFeLFrmHvn?

did you hurt yourself
when you fell from
heaven?

DntUNoMeFrmSumwer?

don't you know me from
somewhere?

DoUBlveInLuv@1stSlt
OrShLIWlkByAgn?

> do you believe in love at
> first sight or shall I walk
> by again?

DoUHavAMpIKEpGtnLstInYaiis?

> do you have a map?
> I keep getting lost in your
> eyes

DoUHavROmInYaBg4MyFeRariKEs?

> do you have room in your
> handbag for the keys to
> my Ferrari?

DoUMndIfIFntsizAbtU?

> do you mind if I fantasize
> about you?

DoUSlEpOnYaStmch&DoUMndIflDo?
do you sleep on your
stomach and do you
mind if I do?

DoUWan2SngOrShldISaSRy?
do you want to snog
or should I apologize?

DoYaiisBthrU-ThABthrMe?
do your eyes bother you?
they bother me

DrpM   drop 'em

DsGodNoHesM$inAn0:-)?
does God know he's
missing an angel?

HABABWan2GtLckE?
> hey baby, want to
> get lucky?

Hrs10p2CLYaPrnts2SaUWntBHOm2nite
> here's 10p to call your
> parents to say you won't
> be home tonight

HrsYaChnc2Gt2NoMe
> here's your chance to
> get to know me

HwDoULkMeSoFa?
> how do you like me
> so far?

HwWosHvnWenULftIt?
> how was heaven when
> you left it?

IdLOkGOdOnU
> I'd look good on you

IfHe/SheDsntShwUpImRtHre
> if he/she doesn't show
> up, I'm right here

**IfISedUHdAButifulBdy
WldUHldItAgnstMe?**
> if I said you had a
> beautiful body would you
> hold it against me?

IfUvLstYaVrgntyCnIHavTBxItCAmIn?

if you've lost your
virginity, can I have the
box it came in?

IHOpUNoCPRCosUTAkMyBrthAwA

I hope you know CPR
'cos you take my breath
away

**ILOkdUpSxyInTDxtnre2DA&
YaNAmWosLstd**

I looked up sexy in the
dictionary today and your
name was listed

ILstMyFOnNoCNIHavYas?

> I lost my phone number.
> Can I have yours?

ImA*vinRtst&IWan2EatU

> I'm a starving artist and
> I want to eat you

ImLOkn4AFrndDoUWan2BMyFrnd?

> I'm looking for a friend.
> Do you want to be my
> friend?

ImNtLOkin4ARltnshplm
LOkin4AnXprnce

> I'm not looking for a
> relationship, I'm looking
> for an experience

ImNuInTwnCnUGveMeDrctns 2YaAprtmnt?

> I'm new in town. Can you give me directions to your apartment?

IMi$MyTeDBerWldUSlEpWivMe?

> I miss my teddy bear. Would you sleep with me?

InMyABCIWldPutU&I2gtha

> in my alphabet I would put you and I together

IsItHotInHreOrIsItU?

> is it hot in here or is it you?

IvBinWtchnUNotWtchnMe

> I've been watching you
> not watching me

IWldDiHaPIfISawUNkdJst1nc

> I would die happy if I
> saw you naked just once

LtsGo2MyPlAc&DoTThngs
ILTLEvry1WeDidNEWA

> let's go to my place and
> do the things I'll tell
> everyone we did anyway

MAIEndThsSntncWivAPropstn?

> may I end this sentence
> with a proposition?

MmmUBrngNuMnin2TWrdEdble

mmm, you bring new
meaning to the word
edible

MyNAmls…BtUCnCaLMeLvr

my name is…
but you can call me lover

NlcDr$CnITlkUOutOfIt?

nice dress, can I talk
you out of it?

PctrThsUMeB%lesx2

picture this – you, me,
bubble baths and
champagne

RUFrE2NiteOrWLItCstMe?
> are you free tonight or
> will it cost me?

RUREd2GoHOmNw?
> are you ready to go
> home now?

RUUP4IT?   are you up for it?

**RYaLgsTrdUvBinRuNinThru
MyMndALNite?**
> are your legs tired?
> You've been running
> through my mind all
> night?

ScrwMeIfImRongBtUWan2XmeDntYa?

screw me if I'm wrong
but you want to kiss me
don't you?

ShLICaLUOrNdgU4Bfst2moro?

shall I call you or nudge
you for breakfast
tomorrow?

SOSImLstWchWA2YaPlAc?

help, I'm lost – which
way to your place?

SRy2StareIWan2RmbaYaFAc4MyDrms

       excuse me, do you mind
       if I stare at you for a
       minute? I want to
       remember your face for
       my dreams

ThtDr$WldLOkGrtOnMyBdrOmFlr

       that dress would look
       great on my bedroom
       floor

ThtsANIc:-)ShAmItsNtALURWarin

       that's a nice smile, shame
       it's not all you are wearing

**ThtOwtFtWldLOkGrtlnACrmpldHpOnMy
BdrOmFlr2moroam**

> that outfit would look
> great in a crumpled heap
> on my bedroom floor
> tomorrow morning

TAkAChncOnMe?

> take a chance on me?

**TWrdOfTdAlsLgs
LtsGo2MyPlAc&SprdTWrd**

> the word of the day is
> 'legs' – lets go to my place
> and spread the word

ULOkLIkTKindaGY/GrlWhsHrdEvryLIn InTBOkSoWots1Mor?

> you look like the kind of
> guy/girl who's heard
> every line in the book,
> so what's one more?

UMstBGrt@ FshnUGotMeHOkLln&Snka

> you must be great at
> fishing – you got me
> hook, line and sinker

URMyCndrLa&ImYaPrnc

> you are my Cinderella
> and I am your prince

URSoHotUMltTPlstcInMyWLT

you're so hot you melt
the plastic in my wallet

URTRsnMn/WmnFLInLuv

you are the reason
men/women fall in love

**WldUBMyLuvBuFASolCnLAUOutOnTTbl
&TAkWotlWan?**

would you be my love
buffet so I can lay you
out on the table and take
what I want?

WldULlkSum12MxWivYaDrnk?

would you like someone
to mix with your drink?

WotCnIDo2MAkUBMIn?
> what can I do to make
> you be mine?

XcusMeCnUGivMeDrctns2Ya<3?
> excuse me, can you
> give me directions to
> your heart?

**XcusMeSRy2BthaUBtIWosWndrinIfThe
rWosNePSibiltyOfASng?**
> excuse me, I'm sorry to
> bother you, but I was
> wondering if there was
> any possibility of a snog?

UT1kin2Me?

You talking to me ?– conversation pieces

(Turn through 90 degrees to read)

:-p?	wassup?
;[ ]?	hungry?
:-D	I am very happy
:->>	a huge smile
*^_^*	a huge dazzling grin
:-[	I am down and unhappy

:-<	I'm sad that you don't want to go out with me
:-]	you will? that's great!
:-I	I couldn't care less actually
>:->	I have just made a really devilish remark
>;->	I have just made a very lewd remark
;-) or P-)	wink, wink, nudge, nudge
>:-)	ooh you devil!

`;-)`	don't hit me for what I just said
`:-Q`	I have no idea what you are talking about
`O:-)`	it was a perfectly innocent reply
`m(_ _)m`	I am so sorry, I bow to your better judgement
`-/-`	sure, I am stirring up trouble
`<*)))-{`	catch me if you can
`:-$`	put your money where your mouth is

:-\	I am not sure this is a good idea
<:-)?	maybe this is a stupid question?
__/~`-'~_/	don't follow your line of thought
O-G-<	me, me, me – is that all you can think about?
:-S	words fail me
:-@	I am shocked
:-O	I am surprised

(@_@)	I am stunned by your boldness
(o_o)	I am shocked by that suggestion
@*&$!%	you know what that means...
:*(@)	you are drunk and shouting
%*@:-(	I am hungover with a headache
<&-I	I feel foolish and tearful

>-::-D	smitten by Cupid's arrow
!:-)	that's imaginative
+++<3+++	I'm infatuated with you
<3	are you a model? I'm star-struck
TEXT	YELLING

CyberChtUp

Internet pick-ups for the really dedicated

CnUOpnMyHot:-Accnt?

can you open my hot
male account?

DoU.comHreOftn?

do you.com here often?

DoUWan2Crsh@MyPlAc?

do you want to crash at
my place?

DntWeJstClk? don't we just click?

URTATchmntIvBinLOkin4
>you are the attachment
>I've been looking for

Wa$aNIcUrILIkUDoinInAPlAcLIkThs?
>what's a nice Url like you
>doing in a place like this?

YaWndWsRLIkiisIn2YaSOl
>your windows are like
>eyes into your soul

YrHOmPAgOrMln?
>your homepage or mine?

51

Cmon+!0r-!?

Come on, yes or no?
Shorthand for quick replies

:-)	ha ha
l-)	hee hee
-D	ho ho
:->	hey hey
:-(	boo hoo
:-l	hmmm

:-O	oops
:-*	ooops
:-o	uh oh!
{}	'no comment'
l:-O	no explanation given
:-o	oh, no!
#:-o	oh, no!
:-0	ohhhhhh!
l:-O	big ohhhhhh!
<:-O	eeek!

:-)))	reeeaaaalllly happy
:-P	nyahhhh!
>;-('	I am spitting mad
:-)~	I am drooling
:-9	I am licking my lips
<3	I love you
:~~(	I am bawling
:-@	I am screaming
:-&	I feel tongue-tied

((H)))	a big hug
:-X	a big wet kiss
I-O	I am bored
:-o zz z z Z Z	I am very bored
o'U	yawning (profile)
:^U	forget it
o'V	shouting (profile)
o'w ?	are you telling me the truth?

:-e	I am disappointed
(:-...	I am heart-broken
:-t	I am cross and pouting
**-(	I am very, very shocked
:^D	great! I like it!
M:-)	respect
:+(	I am hurt by that remark
$->	I am happily excited
=^)	I am open-minded

>w	oh really! (ironic)
8-]	'wow, maaan'
/;-)	do you really think so?
O-S-<	I am in a hurry

ItWrkd4Thm
No 1 love lines

AintLuvABtch?

ain't love a bitch?

Aint2Proud2Bg

ain't too proud to beg

ALAlOnAmI   all alone am I

ALINEdIsYaSwEtLuvin

all I need is your sweet
loving

AlOn?   alone?

AnAFAr2Rmba?
>an affair to remember?

&SoIWLWAt4U
>and so I will wait for you

O:-) angel

BABDnt4getMyNo
>baby don't forget my
>number

BABDntGetHOkdOnMe
>baby don't get hooked
>on me

BABINEdYaLuvin
>baby I need your loving

BABURDynamIt
  baby you are dynamite

BABWeBeTaTry2GetIt2gtha
  baby we better try to get
  it together

BAs1?   be as one?

BeGin   begging

Brn2BWld   born to be wild

BrnBABBrn   burn baby burn

ChAngYaMnd   change your mind

ChOsMe   choose me

CldItBImFaLinInLuv?
could it be I'm falling
in love?

CnITAkUHOmLTleGrl?
can I take you home little
girl?

CnThsBLuv? can this be love?

CntTAkMyiisOFfaU
can't take my eyes off
of you

CnUFEllt? can you feel it?

CnUKiklt ? can you kick it?

CnUPrT? can you party?

CntWAtAnuvaMinit
        can't wait another minute

CumOnHOm   come on home

DArMe?   dare me?

DaYaThnkImSxy?
        do you think I'm sexy?

DnceWivMe?   dance with me?

DntBrngMeDwn
        don't bring me down

DntItMAkUFElGOd?
        don't it make you feel
        good?

DntMAkMeWAt2Lng
>don't make me wait
>too long

DntStndSoClOs2Me
>don't stand so close
>to me

DoIt4Luv   do it for love

DoUBlveInMgic?
>do you believe in magic?

DoUFEILIkIFEl?
>do you feel like I feel?

DoUWanMe?   do you want me?

DoYaDoYaWan2PlsMe?
do you, do you want to
please me

EvryboDNEdsSumBoD2Luv
everybody needs
somebody to love

FElsLIkT1stTlm
feels like the first time

FrEYaBoD free your body

GiMeGiMeGiMeAMnAftaMdnIte
gimme, gimme, gimme a
man after midnight

GiMeSumLuvin
gimme some loving

GivIn2Me   give in to me

GivItUp   give it up

GoNaMAkUnOFaUCntRfUs
   gonna make you an offer
   you can't refuse

Got2GetUIn2MyLIf
   gotta get you into my life

GtIt2gtha   get it together

GtItWIlUCn   get it while you can

GTinReD4Luv   getting ready for love

HaP2gtha?   happy together?

HAU   hey you

HldMe   hold me

ICnMAkUFElGOd
                I can make you feel
                good

ICntGtNoStisfctn
                I can't get no satisfaction

IDdntNoILuvdUTLISawURokNRoL
                I didn't know I loved you
                till I saw you rock and
                roll

IFElLuvCuminOn
                I feel love coming on

IGotUBAb   I got you babe

IJstKEpThnknAboutUBAB

I just keep thinking about you baby

IJstWan2MAkLuv2U

I just want to make love to you

ILTAkUHOm2nite

I'll take you home tonight

ImALUNEd   I'm all you need

ImNotInLuv   I'm not in love

ImQulifd2Stsfy

I'm qualified to satisfy

IMSdTBus I missed the bus

INEdSum1 I need someone

INoWotBysLIk I know what boys like

IRLEWan2CU2nite
I really want to see you
tonight

IsThsALuvThng?
is this a love thing?

IsntItTIm? isn't it time

IWaNaBYaMn I wanna be your man

IWanUINEdUILuvU
I want you, I need you,
I love you

IWdntNrmLyDoThsKindaThng
I wouldn't normally do this kind of thing

JstSANo just say no

KEpMeInMnd keep me in mind

LetItBMe let it be me

LetLuvRUl let love rule

LetMeNo let me know

LetYaLuvFlO let your love flow

LItMyFIr light my fire

LOkWotUStrtd look what you started

LtsGtTTOs let's get tattoos

LtsSpndTNite2gtha
let's spend the night together

LuvLlkARckt love like a rocket

LuvT1URWiv love the one you're with

MABBAB maybe baby

MadAbtU mad about you

MadIfUDnt mad if you don't

MAd2Luv	made to love
MAkItHPn	make it happen
MAkItREl	make it real
MAkItSOn	make it soon
MAkItWivMe	make it with me
MAkLuv2Me	make love to me
MorThnAWmn	
	more than a woman
MoveYaBoD	move your body

NEdU2nite   need you tonight

NEdYaLuvSoBad
> need your love so bad

NETImNEPlAc any time any place

NevaFndALuvLlkThsB4
> never found a love like
> this before

NEWAThtUWanMe
> any way that you want me

NoLmt   no limit

0Is4eva   nothing is forever

1OfThseNites?	one of these nights?
OpnYa<3	open your heart
OUPrTThng	oh you pretty thing
PlEsDntGo	please don't go
PSSblyMAB?	possibly maybe?
ReD4Luv?	ready for love?
ReDOrNot	ready or not
ReD2Go?	ready to go?
RmbaMe?	remember me?

ROLWivIt	roll with it
RsQMe	rescue me
M:-)	respect
Rn2Me	run to me
RnBABRn	run baby run
RSVP	answer please

RUGeTinEnufOfWotMAksUHaP?
are you getting enough
of what makes you
happy?

RULOnsum2Nite?

are you lonesome
tonight?

RURede4Luv are you ready for love?

RUStisfld? are you satisfied

SAUDntMnd say you don't mind

SAULBTher say you'll be there

SAUSAMe say you say me

SAULStAUntl2moro

say you'll stay until
tomorrow

SAUWL say you will

ShIBy	shy boy
SoHreIAm	so here I am
SOS	help
StAWivMeBAB	stay with me baby
StndByMe	stand by me
StsfyMySOl	satisfy my soul
SumLIkItHot	some like it hot
SumThng4TWEknd?	something for the weekend?

SumThngsGoTaHldOfMy<3
something's got a hold of my heart

SwEtTlknGuy sweet talking guy

TAkYaTlm take your time

Tmptd? tempted?

2niteCldBTNIt tonight could be the night

UBlOMyMnd you blow my mind

UGtTLOk you got the look

WAtin4AGrlLIkU
waiting for a girl like you

WeCnWrkItOut we can work it out

WenWLICUAgn?
when will I see you
again?

WerDoWeGoFrmHre?
where do we go from
here?

WevGotItGoinOn
we've got it going on

WamBam? wham bham?

Wlcum2TPlesurDOm
welcome to the pleasure
dome

WotevaGetsUThruTNIt
    whatever gets you
    through the night

WotevaUWan   whatever you want

WotRUWAtin4?
            what are you waiting for?

WotsItLIk2BBUtifl?
            what's it like to be
            beautiful?

WotsLuvGot2DoWivIt?
            what's love got to
            do with it?

WotsYaNAmWotsYaNo?
        what's your name?
        what's your number?

UREvrEThng2Me
        you are everything to me

URT1   you are the one

UvGotIt   you've got it

UvGotMyNoYDntUUseIt?
        you've got my number,
        why don't you use it?

YaBoDsCLin   your body's calling

YaMamaWntLIkMe
        your mama won't like me

YaTImIsGNaCum
        your time is gonna come

YuMEYuMEYuME
        yummy, yummy, yummy

YumYumGiMeSum
        yum, yum give me some

YungFrE&Sngl
        young, free and single

Bak2YaR0ts

**Basic acronyms & abbreviations
for fast talkers**

AAM	as a matter of fact
AB	ah bless!
AFAIC	as far as I'm concerned
AFAIK	as far as I know
AKA	also known as
ASAP	as soon as possible

ATB	all the best
B	be
BBFN	bye bye for now
BCNU	be seeing you
B4	before
BFN	bye for now
BRB	be right back
BTW	by the way
Bwd	backward
BYKT	but you knew that

C	see
CMIIW	correct me if I'm wrong
CU	see you
CYA	see you
Doin	doing
EOL	end of lecture
FAQ	frequently asked question(s)
FITB	fill in the blank
F2T	free to talk

Fwd	forward
FWIW	for what it's worth
FYI	for your information
GG	good game
GoNa	going to
Gr8	great
HAND	have a nice day
H8	hate
HTH	hope this/to help(s)
IAC	in any case

IAE	in any event
ICL	in Christian love
IDK	I don't know
IIRC	if I recall correctly
IMCO	in my considered opinion
IMHO	in my humble opinion
IMNSHO	in my not so humble opinion
IMO	in my opinion
IOW	in other words

ITYFIR	I think you'll find I'm right
IYDKIDKWD	if you don't know I don't know who does
IYKWIM	if you know what I mean
IYKWIMAITYD	if you know what I mean and I think you do
IYSS	if you say so
JM2p	just my 2 pennyworth
L8	late
L8r	later
Luv	love

LOL	lots of luck or laughing out loud
MGB	may God bless
MHOTY	my hat's off to you
MMDP	make my day punk!
Mob	mobile
MSg	message
MYOB	mind your own business
NE	any
NE1	anyone

NH	nice hand
NO1	no one
NRN	no reply necessary
OTOH	on the other hand
PCM	please call me
PLS	please
PPL	people
PS	post script
R	are
ROTF	rolling on the floor

ROTFL	rolling on the floor laughing
RU?	are you?
RUOK?	are you OK?
SIT	stay in touch
SITD	still in the dark
SMS	short message service
SOME1	someone
StrA	stray
SWG	scientific wild guess

THNQ	thank you
TIA	thanks in advance
TIC	tongue in cheek
Ti2GO	time to go
TPTB	the powers that be
TWIMC	to whom it may concern
TUVM	thank you very much
U	you
UR	you are
WAN2	want to

WAN2TLK?	want to talk?
W/	with
W	without
Wknd	weekend
WRT	with respect to
WTTW	word to the wise
YKWYCD	you know what you can do
YMMV	your mileage may vary (you may not have the same luck I did)

YA	your
YWIA	you're welcome in advance
1	one
1dafL	wonderful
2	to, too
2day	today
2moro	tomorrow
2nite	tonight
3sum	threesome

4	for
\<G\>	grinning
\<J\>	joking
\<L\>	laughing
\<O\>	shouting
\<S\>	smiling
\<Y\>	yawning
$	double s
T	the